P9-CMW-402

The American Poetry Review/Honickman
First Book Prize

The Honickman Foundation is dedicated to the support of projects that promote spiritual growth and creativity, education and social change. At the heart of the mission of the Honickman Foundation is the belief that creativity enriches contemporary society because the arts are powerful tools for enlightenment, equity and empowerment, and must be encouraged to effect social change as well as personal growth. A current focus is on the particular power of photography and poetry to reflect and interpret reality, and, hence, to illuminate all that is true.

The annual American Poetry Review/Honickman First Book Prize offers publication of a book of poems, a $3,000 award, and distribution by Copper Canyon Press through Consortium. Each year a distinguished poet is chosen to judge the prize and write an introduction to the winning book. The purpose of the prize is to encourage excellence in poetry, and to provide a wide readership for a deserving first book of poems. *Things Are Happening* is the inaugural book in the series.

Things Are Happening

Things Are Happening

POEMS BY

JOSHUA BECKMAN

WINNER OF THE APR/HONICKMAN

FIRST BOOK PRIZE

The American Poetry Review

PHILADELPHIA

811
Bec

Copyright © 1998 by Joshua Beckman.
All rights reserved.
Printed in the United States of America.
No part of this book may be used or reproduced
in any manner whatsoever without written permission
except in the case of brief quotations embodied in
critical articles and reviews.

Direct all inquiries to
The APR/Honickman First Book Prize
The American Poetry Review
1721 Walnut Street
Philadelphia, PA 19103

Distribution by Copper Canyon Press/Consortium

Library of Congress Catalogue Card Number: 98-71446

ISBN 0-9663395-0-9 (cloth, alk. paper)
ISBN 0-9663395-1-7 (pbk., alk. paper)

First edition

Designed by Cynthia Krupat

The author wishes to thank the Edward Albee Foundation,
the Montalvo Center for the Arts, and the Ludwig Vogelstein
Foundation; Nedge, Response, and Permeable Press,
where a number of these poems first appeared;
and his family and friends who were his support
while he wrote this book.

Contents

Introduction

BY GERALD STERN

What attracts me to Joshua Beckman's poetry is the unique ability he has of combining a classically simple vocabulary, a lucid poetic syntax, and a highly available and dramatic subject matter in such a way that not only is there a poetic tension generated but a peculiar and original vision as well. Perhaps the easiest thing to talk about is his "voice," ambiguous a term as that is. This voice is direct, clear, modest, wondrous, affectionate, hopeful. Even courageous. And tenacious. It is simultaneously grounded, and deeply grounded, in the language of and the poetic approach of that group of poets we tend to identify as the New York School, and the language and psychology of a young poet who came of age in the 1990's, with all the interests and passions that such a poet might have.

"New York School" is a delightfully unreasonable term that includes not only the likes of such New Yorkers as Schuyler, Ashbery and O'Hara, but a great many west-coasters and even a couple New Jerseyans and Pennsylvanians. Grandfather Carlos, we might remember, only visited the canyons from his perch in Rutherford. It is always a joyful piece of detective work to smell out the sources in a young poet, both elected sources and sources, if you will, in spite of him or herself. Schuyler is here a little, and O'Hara with a vengeance, but also Spicer and Lorca and Whitman and Berrigan and Hart Crane. And Creeley and Snyder and Zukofsky and a little Roethke, and a little Mandelstam. Even a little Pound, though only the language and the form, none of the paranoid melodrama.

I think I am more interested, however, in how Beckman is not a New York poet, how he strays from the mark and asserts his own individuality. It is a delicate point here, but I think he is different in the direct, non-ironic, and passionate expression of emotion, and in the use of a language that is not special, symbolic, scholarly, exclusionary, digressive, arch, or encoded. Indeed, it is inclusiveness and openness that characterizes his poetry. What caused me to notice it, and why it is so original, is his ability, which can hardly be described analytically, to create aesthetic tension and at the same time to give pleasure — and heart — to the reader and to move him so. Book after book crosses my desk where the poet proclaims him or herself by various acts of non-musical and muddy incoherence. Beckman takes the more difficult road.

His poems — at least the ones I've seen — are narrative or meditative journeys that reflect, and reflect upon, the mythical musings of the idealized narrator and journeyer. They don't do this deliberately. They are not self-conscious efforts to reproduce Campbell or Jung-like versions of a certain kind of mythical encounter or consciousness. Thank God! Rather, they are figurative or metaphysical encounters done with concrete and ordinary language whereby the literal in itself becomes symbolic. I don't mean that the poetry is symbolical, the way deep image poetry was, or that what he says is not to be taken seriously — and literally — for its own sake. It's just that his mind works in such a way, or his heart, that the literal becomes, at once, figurative and representative. And this is where he breaks from the New York School, or most of it.

I think he is a visionary poet, by which I mean he is in touch with something tenuous, and that he feels the other voice or the other thing inside him. His virtue here is that his geography is common, and he is too studious of his own route to be dithering or magisterial or magical. Also he is modest, trusting, and noncombative. If he is visionary it is not a particular vision he is disclosing. He is not ideological. He is visionary the way Hart Crane was. And he doesn't base that vision on rejection.

"Old Watermelon Hands" is a case in point. On the one hand, it is a biographical sketch of an old man "from the islands" who works a little magic and gathers our passionate attention, and on the other hand he is helpless, bumbling, and literally falling apart. He is "rotten" and has a "sour look for everyone." He is a kind of uncle, a kind of entertainer, a mysterious stranger, a caretaker. He knows our thoughts — yet he is truly, literally, a melon, especially his hands:

> He shook his hands in the air
> making sloshing sounds
> that were supposed to let me know
> that he was more than ripe.
> I thought he had become kinder
> and wanted to tell him
> that he had gone soft.

. . . .

Watermelon Hands would cook a good meal
and put the kids to bed.
While I slept he would fill me with dreams
of insufficiency and illness,
he would suck the strength out of my body,
my lips ending like dried tomatoes.
He would bang around the house,
a last check on everything . . .

He is Shapeshifter, Mentor and Trickster. He is those things; but he's never an
abstraction.

Or "Purple Heart Highway." The journey here is not only that beloved
one that Steinbeck, Kerouac, Wolfe and dozens of others embarked on in their
searches for adventure, excitement and experience, but the parallel journey for
unity, spirituality and understanding that accompanies the other. It is a paean
to motion, and to the automobile, of all things. Yet it is strangely fresh, as if
Beckman were the first, or as if it never occurred to him that he wasn't.

I fell asleep on the road
ended up half in the woods, half in the way,
two wheels off the ground like a cartoon.
Now I think it is good just to be alive.
. . . .

Picked up two boys on their way to the beach.
You always liked picking up hitchhikers,
said it was near to a kiss
said it was mystery,
never know what will hop out of the woods
once you stop.
But the boys are quiet
Young thin boys

in the back seat of the car
all the way to sugar beach
. . . .

I walk around until it is morning
and get the times from a drug store
Fall asleep two blocks from the beach
one leg in the way of a bakery.
Some tiny percentage of sand in the street
the infrequent sound of waves
unmistakably, salt in the air . . .
. . . .

My car, piece by piece
is taken away by swift young men
who treasure it, the way you'd treasure a lung . . .

The most interesting poem—for me—is the last, and, I believe, the latest, one, "Winter's Horizon." It is a peculiar combination of narrative and lyric, barely broken up, barely distinguished by parts or sections, certainly not lettered or numbered, so that one thing flows into another and the time-line is not necessarily sequential. It is a family romance, with twin boys—three years old, I think, in the imagining, a sister, a dear father, and a troubled mother. There seems to be an ominous event at the center of things, which provides the tension and the connection. It is really, though, just a hint of something, perhaps a fire, perhaps just neglect. And a ruined house is the issue. Though there is no grand tragic event depicted. The poem therefore is mostly meditative and held together by the language and the haunted memory of the speaker.

Here is the father:

inspired father
yellow sun
starting up
in the garage

                    appearing on its own
            God bless your father
        everyone runs quickly
                            to the porch
                pushing at the mesh windows
        our bodies waving good-bye
            God bless our father
            God bless him
                and God bless
                    the two thousand dollar
                bit of security
                    that motors him around

The mother:

        Your mother stares out
        of the fuzzy police-camera part of your brain,
        says look, I was just waiting for the fucker to come back.
        Sure it was funny at first, ha ha, but come on.
        I start thinking we've got half a dozen kids
        and yell yell yell the next thing I know
        I'm hypnotized
        Stuff shooting out of the side
        Grass looking new as Christmas
        My man inching away
        The wake closing like something at the end of a movie
        and I start thinking the most honest
        sort of cherishable thoughts
        like how I love all you kids
        enough to send you off that way
        and how the beautiful circumstances
        of grass washing after

of trails leading towards
will make easy
all the difficult
comings and goings.

The brothers:

This is the sort of peace we ask for
and the sort of peace, at times, we deserve,
but you buy the kid a cheap sweater because what the hell
he's going to outgrow it in six months anyway
and the next thing you know he's just an inch too close
to the fire and fwoom, a kind of harmless flash from every
little loose end runs from bottom to top of him
and then goes out just as quick
scaring the hell out of his well-meaning three-year-old brother
who chases him around the room
just trying to get the damn sweater off.

Beckman's language has none of the high style about it, whether of Stevens, Crane or Ashbery. It is certainly closest to O'Hara, though the posture is entirely different. It is not only plain speech but it is common speech, and if the style is slant or askew the language, as such, never is. It's as if he trusted what was said in his living room and did not have to reconstitute it. It is a continuation and development of the two-hundred-year-old tradition.

Beckman's character, his imprint, which includes but is larger than his voice, which includes but is larger than his moral and aesthetic position—I can only characterize as tender, reverential, trusting, sane. It is not innocent but it is believing. It is not naive but it is hopeful. It is not pessimistic but it is painfully realistic. There is form, diction, subject matter, language, and music, but it is this imprint, this *print*, that captures us. If I had to give a name to it—for Beckman— I would call it *affection*. His identity is through affection. That is his print.

Things Are Happening

Lament for the Death of a Bullfighter

FOR DAVID AVIDAN

1

At the news of your death
children could hold back their giggling no more
and fits of laughter spread like chicken pox
all over this country
and at first no one noticed
because kids are always doing stuff like that,
but soon there was no stopping them
no quieting them down at all
and then the sky turned dark
and authority slunk away
like the man who never wanted to be sheriff
and the kids stayed outside
floating down the streets in boats made from junk
and when the moon showed up
they finally went in
left their soaking clothes at the door
and headed straight for their computers.
And then we had lost them to you
their eyes glued to the screen
their fragile hearts pumping with electric blood
their thousand little thumbs
frantically bouncing up and down.

2

At the news of your death
pardon me, the mail is slow from there to here,
a giant wave finally reached our country
and sat his big gray body down
next to the few people left

who hadn't run away in fear
(again like the movies)
and the wave told such a captivating
intercontinental story that we didn't notice
him turning to mud like an ice cream cone
and when we looked, all that was left
were a dozen pie-shaped jellyfish,
but the ocean took those back quickly,
before any trouble got started.

3

At the news of your death
the computers at the phone company
all over New York City
and the surrounding area
went on strike
and had to be replaced
with people,
who made every connection
and answered every question,
much to the surprise of the callers
who had become accustomed to automation,
and no matter how many people called
(and once the lonely bachelors found out
there were a lot)
everything went smooth as could be
due to the courtesy and stealth of those young operators
and although things got back to normal the next day
—no reflection on you—
more than a few romances
budded from the sparks of that confusion.

4

At the news of your death
couples who had never heard of you
kept walking
and were only dragged back
by the nagging sensation
that after hundreds of miles
they had left homes and families unattended.
And one source stated
that a woman in her early thirties
after returning and finding that she
had not left her oven on,
headed directly back out
and has not been heard from since.

5

At the news of your death
in every hospital in America
and all at once
babies were born
and then slapped on the butt,
and preschoolers woke up early from their naps
and the more the teachers yelled
and snapped their red rulers
the more riled up the little ones became.
At home, all they would have for dinner was chocolate milk
and they threw their pajamas out the window
and snuck dirty books to bed
and the next day everyone wore
their crusty fake mustaches to school

and answered their teacher's questions
in rhyme.

6

At the news of your death
not a good poem was written
not in your country or mine
not by any of the famous poets from anywhere,
no, we all just sat down and had a good cry,
even the ones who didn't think so much of you
got up from their chairs, misty,
thinking it was their wives or their age
or the millennium
and no matter what we did,
none of us could get back to it,
not for a good long while.

7

At the news of your death
everyone turned on the TV
and left the room
at the news of your death
everyone took pictures
that would come out blurry
at the news of your death
every dinner, no matter curried or cajun,
came out sweeter, unbelievably sweeter
than anyone could have imagined.

8

At the news of your death
on the day that you died
the paper came with a little note
saying that you were a crazy and good man,
which I knew
and that you were a talented poet
with thirty books to your credit,
which I knew
and saying that you were dead,
so I went out and threw it in the street.
Later the neighbors would mention it
and I would get sad, and wouldn't explain,
and I expect it will be a point of contention for a while.

9

David, at the news of your death
the trees became sad,
not all of them of course,
but a few in every country,
and they decided to skip summer
and drop their leaves right then
and despite confusion on the ground,
birds in naked nests, and wind with nothing to do
all over the world they have proposed to keep this up.
You see, being trees they can't believe you're not coming back.
They say they will do this year after year,
stubborn and ignorant trees that they are.
They have promised to keep this up, David,

despite official protest and calm pleading of every kind.
Yes, they are determined to keep this up
until you return.

My Story

My story is that I will not be able to eat for days.
His story is that he turned to put groceries in his truck
and the one-year-old floated helplessly through the parking lot
until it hit a brand new pontiac, the kid jumping
at least two inches into the visible morning.
Everyone's story is about the pavement at the supermarket
(the way it smells, when redone, of leaking oil).
My dad's story is that as a kid in Bridgeport you couldn't
afford gum, so people (no joke) chewed roof tar and liked it.
The neighbor's story is that in 1996 the poor still look good
with scars and tattoos and boys still want toughness to be
in their fathers, big as anything.

When I moved into this place the guy downstairs could hear
the couch knocking against the wall as I struggled
to bring it up myself, and came out. Another time he helped
with a bookcase and Dee thought he was drunk. He just has
an odd way of smiling, I told her and when she said hello,
as she left, he lifted his arm. He has an odd way with that too
and never says anything. The kind of guy you imagine hurt
as a kid and now grown used to it (the way we expect the slow
to have grown used to their pace). Sometimes I will see him
in the neighborhood. James said, he walks so purposefully.
Two days ago, when I went right by him on my bike, I saw
the beginnings of a mustache (something else that requires
a certain degree of purpose).

Jon's story was that he lived with us for months
and never told us anything.

Once I saw a man, waiting for his wife, lean on a car
with a car alarm. Those things are so sensitive. The poor baby

started one going and eight-year-old Joseph (next door)
started one with a hose, cleaning his mother's car.
Parents (now I'm thinking of the man again) will remember
how things were much more firm in the old days.
Jon would rush through the living room. You could smell the smoke.
Sometimes he would sit in the car in the driveway and fight
with his girlfriend. Then the two of them would come through
the house. One day she told us that she studied animals
and that she believed this gave her insight into people.

The lemming's story is much more complex than it is made out to be.
Lemmings fight against many things.
When it is cold, lemmings fight for warmth.
When there is no food, lemmings will search for food.
Although they cannot sense affection, there is a feeling
of closeness, a fondness, not unlike love, that lemmings feel
when lemming parents return to the nest.

On a day like today (sunny but mild)
anyone could suggest to you a better way of living
without making you mad. What does your story have to do
with my life is something that a lot of people wonder.
Not everyone has dropped their child.
Not everyone has abandoned hope of forgiveness for a tiny speck
of a thing they were once guilty of.
And not everyone has focused all of their usable energy
on a task as basic as buying an ice cream cone.

But watch how simple it is to make anything complex:
The vanilla and chocolate (swirl) of ice cream getting on
to the outside of the face, the salt and pepper hair
of old age now forming a mustache worth its name

and everything mixed together until that whale, the tongue,
cleans the surface with an awfully belly-strong leap.

Mr. Alves's story could be that the red rose bush lasted
for so much longer than the white rose bush (now three years)
and that the white rose bush is so gone (in such a short time)
that two very young tomato plants live where it lived,
or that the rotten kids who play ball around here
and the rough ears of kale that fill the dirt patch out front
are not and will never be partners in any sense, but instead
it is his story that you grow up five children (three boys
two girls) and even when you are going to be 87 in a month
they never visit or take care of the house, because it does
not make them happy.

Arthur's story is that he was killed at work, an okay
cash settlement turning the poorness of his family's life
into a more complex and emotionally confusing poorness.

One man's story begins with firecrackers and another's begins
with loneliness. There are so many children who grow up
without fathers and so many explanations for this. One boy
will learn to cook. One boy will learn to steal. And one boy
will learn to love anything that comes his way. Today I am
a woman in a bar and he loves me. Later I am the sweet smell
of basil in the air and he loves me. Finally I am the left
feathers of disease and he loves me (so full of regret).

Yesterday Freud was suggesting the father as a certain point
of focus in a young man's life. A point both like and unlike
anyone else. You have children and do your best to keep them.
My dad did a little Buster Keaton to stop my sister from crying

one night and fell off the stairs. Sometimes we fall off the
stairs for our children. That is how much we love our children
he might say. He might say you never leave your children,
no matter what, and if he said this it would be a passionate
pronouncement of what is in his mind.

My sister's story is that she fades away like something
that started out of sight and continues to drift.
In conversation, she will absentmindedly take more than one side
and in bath tubs she will displace only the smallest fraction of water.

For this, the therapist, the nutritionist, and all of our friends
have a story, but none can compare to the wisp of a story
my sister tells. Once we were sitting around and my mother began
to cry. She said "What is it? What is it? What is it?"

There is a trick where one person holds a dollar bill in the air
and another, with fingers poised around it, tries to catch the bill
once it is let go. It is not impossible, but relies solely on luck.
When we see the trick we become aware of the body's limitations.
This is my sister's story. It is as if with one hand she lets go
of the dollar (over and over) and with the other she waits always,
as if for good luck which will never come.

Your story is that you have too much money. When you see something
you like, you buy it. When you have a memory of a particular
moment of childhood, it might not be fond, but it is never difficult,
the way digging a hole is difficult, after the first few feet.
You sometimes believe that a story is better with action.
One story is of a boy who is hit by his father when his father
is not busy hitting his mother. This is a real story (a real bad
story) about someone we know. You could never tell that person

about the window, how you left it open and a wasp got in,
stung your mother on the arm, blew her up like a balloon, someone
saying your mother could have died. Such a little thing
with so much power.

Someone told you to do what you needed to do, to do what makes you
happy, but if you told that story to the boy he might beat you up.
Irony is always that way, humorous. Not necessarily ha ha funny,
but always comical. We smile into the brilliant windows of stores
only to find our teeth glowing and advertised like crooked plates.

What happens when your child whittles herself away to nothing?
What happens when the rock of oblivion falls on your son's head
and kills him because he's black?
What happens when a daughter finds that little stash of resistance
you were saving for yourself and uses it?

Do you stand there in all your darkness prying up the floor
of your life, until it is a pile of boards and nails, recognizably
tall and defiant, or do you float away letting others fend for themselves?
I say, float away. See how far you get. Say to your children
that you will write them from the fruit blue island of your escape.
Say it and they will picture a beach covered with walruses,
thick-toothed dopey walruses, not what you had in mind at all,
but children have a sort of mystical power, the kind that sends you
to the island of someone else's choosing.

Watch what the granddaughter does to her mother's mother's hair,
sticking dandelions into it and without notice if today is your day
to be grandmother, your hair will be full of flowers. Ask the children
to take them out and the air will be just as full of laughter.

You want me to say that all the children will drift away
like balsa-wood planes and you will be the most feminine
version of David or the most masculine version of Mary
watching them move off the mountain until you are the stone
top of it, the air whistling through every turn of oh-so-
complex you. You want me to say that one day a wave
of togetherness will rush everyone to the water, by way
of the wonderful edge of the cliff, something (so different,
like a color you have never seen) occupying the last living room
of your mind. You want me to say that every man, woman, and child
will be hit by their own particular anvil of prejudice,
flattening them like coins, bringing them to a density that even
the most valiant of us have not dreamt.

But my story is simple. A hunger takes hold of me. I become
irrational. I reach wildly for things. I see myself in the
reflection of a window. I call my mother. She says that I
should never have left my family. I call my children. They are
understanding. They are like Mr. Alves. They say we must do
what makes us happy. This is my story.

Ode to Old Watermelon Hands

Old Watermelon Hands sped into town
broken foot crooked on the accelerator
and a stiff back from driving
or being dead and almost forgotten.

Watermelon Hands rung in the new year
with a grapefruit necklace
and a sour look for everyone.

He followed me into the office
walking sorely on two sleeping legs.
Put a little hole in one of those
big hands of his
setting a slanted mirror straight.

I ignored him because he was a rotten man
when he was alive.
I kept my head down
looking at things on my desk
and he came forward saying "Do you know
what you're doing? Do you know what you're doing?"
He was caught up in a world of paternity,
unwittingly slapping a cake around
because it wouldn't rise.
He was rehearsing memories and suggesting
well-equipped phrases of redemption.
Very simply,
he was looking at me,
but he was looking at the wrong man.

2

Banging his crazy hands on my desk,
working his elbows in a red fit,
he knocked so heavily that nearly all
of his left melon came flying off
leaving a white chip poking out of his wrist
like a cut of glass in a hand
and the other one broke in two,
leaning a bowl-sized piece
right up against me.

It was not surprising
that this is how he was
stumbling in after death
looking lazily over me
mistaking my life
for the completion of my youth.

Going from life to death
and death to here
seemed only to reinforce
his old false notions about distance,
about the distance between two points,
it seemed only to empower
his blind and grave
momentum.

3

Then, he was quiet,
and as I looked up

a pink river watered my papers.
It was not like him at all,
this sad emptied expression,
and there he lost his balance
leaning forward onto the desk
starting a crack in his better hand.

He looked at me slowly
and my mouth began to water.
I wanted to take him
to open his arm like a picnic.
I wanted to hold him still
and peel him apart,
but he was married
and could see it in my eyes,
scooped up the piece in front of me
stabbed the piece in the corner of the room
and was gone.

4

Old Watermelon Hands
spent the night at the neighbors
out on the couch
his eyes and body
like a Thanksgiving uncle.

They took a liking to him
and patched him up with what they had.
I could see him through their window,
laughing and awkwardly gesturing
with his bandaged melons

and everyone was drinking over there
and he was probably telling them stories
about me, when he knew me,
about foolish mistakes and my personality.
He was giving a very lopsided view,
the weight of complications firmly on me,
the historical memory shoveled into my body,
a body that lost its wife
and doesn't care for its youth,
a body like a pair of shoes
over a pair of shoes.

5

I saw him leave
and the neighbors will never
look at me the same way again.
They will probably tell other neighbors
and smile knowing smiles
at my wife in the supermarket.

I could see them kissing and cleaning,
shaking their heads as if it was too much,
yes, too much, about that neighbor,
the neighbor they never really understood.

And soon Watermelon Hands had found the door
to my dark house and was downstairs with the lights off
playing the piano like the beginning of a movie
crashing on keys like a bag full of elbows
throwing music in every corner of the house
and the kids were all teeth and dreams,

charmed out of their beds
like snakes out of baskets.

6

Old Watermelon Hands told me
that I lack any real talent
for setting tables or having children,
that the knives were crooked
and the kids like their mother.

His hands seemed to be healing,
white lines pushing up
a strange map around them,
and the dog chased him through the house
showing off its leather tongue.

Watermelon Hands
disciplined the kids regularly
and I began to feel weak.
He turned from his soap opera
and said that my wife left me
because I didn't know how to love.

I wanted to tell him that he was all wrong
but he had come to me,
my slow and defensive side showing,
when yelling wouldn't get me anywhere
and so he made himself comfortable
in the guest room and on the couch
in front of the mirror and in the backyard.

He was getting old
and it had become hard to turn on him.

7

I couldn't work
and Old Watermelon Hands
was entertaining the kids again.
They were laughing and laughing
singing songs from his island home
making up words
to go with his tangled notes.

He was speaking in an odd language
about his mother, the school teacher,
who would rap his hands with a ruler,
who, he explained, was a large woman
able to scare boys off fences
and animals out of the yard

but who provided him with the most
precise education
the most delicate blend of fine vocabulary
and common sense

and as the children listened
a song rolled like gum balls from their mouths
a song came from their necks and their glands
a song found its humming-winged way into the room
and it was a beautiful song,
it was a song about mothers.

8

Watermelon Hands told the kids
to come in and watch TV.
He walked around the yard
testing for lightning.
He put his hands on the pillow
and made me touch the scars
because they were acting up
because they bulged and pulsed
at the first sign of rain.

When he was outside he knew
and could feel the cold air move across them
and his eyes started to tear.
While I was tracing the scars
on the melons in his lap,
all selfish tenderness,
I told him that when my wife was pregnant
she knew if it was going to snow
and the women got a kick out of it,
but we waited and waited
to have a second child.

9

Watermelon Hands
banged around the shower
once the kids were gone
and surprised me in the living room,
all melons and belly,
dripping from his hair and his penis.

I helped him on with his clothes
wanting to touch the old dark skin
loose under his chest.

He watched me button his shirt
and said that he was not meant for winter.
He shook his hands in the air
making sloshing sounds
that were supposed to let me know
that he was more than ripe.
I thought he had become kinder
and wanted to tell him
that he had gone soft.

10

He talked warmly about island life
and fell asleep on the couch.

I watched his chest move up and down,
anchored by giant fruit,
and soon I wanted to free him,
break off his melons at the wrists.
I wanted to roll them out into the yard
and get the kids to watch him released from gravity.
I imagined his hands snapping off,
leaving important asparagus arms.

But, when I did it,
he was tired and brittle
and one cracked nearly to the elbow
and the other lost a piece,

starting an uncontrollably fast dripping,
and soon I had torn him all the way open
exposing the seeded inside of a shoulder
and all the time trying to even things out.

When the children woke me
the couch was soaked
and Old Watermelon Hands
was in the kitchen
dropping dishes
and yelling something
about me talking
in my sleep.

11

Watermelon Hands would cook a good meal
and put the kids to bed.
While I slept he would fill me with dreams
of insufficiency and illness,
he would suck the strength out of my body,
my lips ending like dried tomatoes.
He would bang around the house,
a last check in on everything
and when I woke he would be gone,
his body like a kid's game
of how to look at the stars for too long.
And I would feel the heavy weight
of giant bulbs planted within me,
their hollow thin rattle
adding up to something awful.
When I stood up

they would sink,
crushing nerves like springs,
crushing all the bones
and settling on my feet,
and before I knew it, they would start again
down my neck and through my shoulders,
like panic or the promise of a life without rest,
making their metallic way past a net of veins,
pushing their lonely bloated rusty way
through my arms and past my wrists.

Purple Heart Highway

1

Frank
bee between flowers
soft light hidden in sunlight
current of warm air
appearing and disappearing
moving through heaven
like the thinnest of fish,
you have left me where a house might fall
where a train might mistakenly come
where the roots of things
watch their trees
taken by wind
blown off as easily as hats
and I can find no consolation
in this tired and reckless wandering.
I find only the moving road of bad conditions,
the fastest lanes, the most stranded shoulders.

2

The signs are off
knocked down by wind
the wooden parts twisted and bent
cars along the highway
a group of men
the hood of their station wagon smoking and open
some bulbs for a drive-in knocked out by kids
neon getting weak and uneven all over
my car not up to snuff,

putting along, bad knocking
when I accelerate.

Open the windows
and turn off the radio.
Sound of the ground.
Sound of the failing engine.
Sound of the split section of town
closing in on me.
Can't see where I am heading
or if I any longer have the means to get there.

3

One day you are like an animal.
You have a routine.
There are certain places that attract you
and others that repel you
and the next you are a kite
at the mercy of every slight tide of wind
forced into quick decisions,
your string attached to the hand of a stranger
your body moving wildly, your heart batted around
by the fastest notes of indecision
and the sky and the world still, unbreakable,
a gray grinning calmness
from which you can get nothing to wake.

4

Down at the beach
early this morning

the surfers and then lightning
brought them in on their bellies
men washing up on shore
I guess we've all had dreams like that.
Then Frank shows up
off the back part of the beach,
an angel in every landscape,
drawing them in
with his warm steadiness.

He is the scientific talk
of the even sounds of rain
and when I reach the parking lot
he has painted everything
the right color of memory.
Sand the color sand was.
Water the color it will always be,
and they are huddled around him
bent over like flowers
surfboards about the beach
as if they peeled off trees
a minute before.

5

One day a man will point to my wheel
having gone flat over the long ride
and I will be forced to leave my car
sandwiched between gravity and the ground
and when I return to it,
something about its helpless kneeling
will cause a reaction in me

not unlike what happens to children
who grow up removed from their parents.

I will want to lift it magically
into the air, its belly exposed like a crab,
a wonderful sense of shade and relief
as it grows smaller and smaller.
I will believe for a moment
that we can be like pears or radishes,
wild, vibrant, full of life,
but calm and at ease
with our immediate and uncontrollable futures.

6

What is certain is that the disappearance
of anything is dreadful, stuffed with anxiety.
That the unbalanced life is far worse
than the good or bad lives.
That the tragic and comic dreams
of falling and climbing
are more desirable than the dreams
of mirrors and puzzles.

I fell asleep on the road
ended up half in the woods, half in the way,
two wheels off the ground like a cartoon.
Now I think it is good just to be alive.
Now I can laugh about it.
But I woke up to a plate full of no options
echoing through the cupped ear of my life,

spinning the wheels that wouldn't,
for anything, take me away.

7

Sometimes I wish for people
to come in through every window
the place full of them
their bodies with the softness
of eggs in cake
and sometimes I wish to be
that harmless splinter
at the tree's deep center,
a sand inching its way
happily to China.

8

I woke up on someone's couch
and wanted not to be alone,
especially thought my legs were cold
without someone else's.

Wanted to be back,
air running through the place
sound of the highway
you filling the kitchen with smoke
and with loneliness,
that sense of doom with us,
so there it is like a neck
presented to the mouth.

Who was it who said,
I want to see you here
at least enough to know that you are gone,
well then give me him instead.

Free his mouth behind bars
and it will never forget you.

9

Coldness without blankets.
Coldness and dreams of coldness
moving in and out of my thinly covered life
the clock filling the room a drop at a time
and when I woke up to the yellow of street lights
and the gray of midnight I wanted to feel a certain way
about friendships, I wanted to feel that I was getting older
and that they are meaning more to me, but with the swiftness
of a year slipping by, I have returned to that thin slot
of my life, that wallet of confusion, enough to keep you
bent over the dirtiness of your house, and separated
from the road that leads to the easy breathing
of the lung's lightest dream.

10

I wanted to see you again
leaving down the driveway
your head like a ball
in that helmet
and potholes and rain
so I watched for you a while

the puddles and the dog
coming up to you
your helmet loosening
tilting to one side
an ear exposed like a clam
slowly moving to the far away
string of street.

For months and even now
I want to play it back
reeling you in to the bottom of the house
magnetic and charming
with dogs running backwards
out of the picture
and then returning.

You toward me
as uneven as ever,
a man like children
lopsided like a potato

a handful of you
swept away like love.

11

When I was young
they put a school teacher in a space shuttle
and shot her off to forever.

All boys dream of the moon,
even if they don't want to go there.

We saw fuel tanks drop silently
from the sides of a rocket,
quiet as the first moment of lightning,
their drift, their airiness,
we saw an explosion
a trail of smoke
clear as an isolated intestine
and it was less peculiar
less odd, less simple,
the way a disconnected side-car
will drift simply off a cliff.
It was not impossible,
this small family of heroes
burning up.

It was not unlikely or unbalancing,
the way that a successful trip to the moon,
its weightlessness, its scientific complexity,
its willing abandon, is forever unbalancing
to the ones who watch it go.

12

Picked up two boys on their way to the beach.
You always liked picking up hitchhikers,
said it was near to a kiss
said it was mystery,
never know what will hop out of the woods
once you stop.
But the boys are quiet
young thin boys
in the back seat of the car

all the way to sugar beach
and I am scared of what sadness
convinces one to do,
a tongue rolling over a routine
of questions for strangers,
and them still as apples in a bag.

13

People are gone
they come and are gone
sometimes they bring the blues with them
sometimes they turn off like lights
sometimes they are spilling over
or bottled up like a car
full of teenagers
about to find the accidental edge
of the world
past your house
the electricity of sweaters
a wide laughing voice
the smoothest
most balled up piece of paper
between someone else's hands
then, rushing high overhead.

14

I became uneasy
with the notions of health and permanency.
I went to the aquarium and realized
that the fish were not drowning,

were not suffocating,
but that they were free to lounge
on the sandy bottom
or drift slowly through the completeness
of their clearly visible lives.

You see in movies
the image of breaking glass
of water pouring everywhere
of the fish's unique and tragic suffering
alive in moist well-furnished rooms,
but it is never that way.

A crazy man broke into the Mystic Aquarium
and tried to free the sharks with a three foot mallet.
Almost comic, how tired he became, how they dragged him away,
how the fish barely noticed, how he woke up alive
and unrelieved, human, completely unbruised.

15

I am just now learning things about myself.
How I run myself into the ground.
How I tire myself out, make myself go on
nothing for days.

I don't know if others are like this,
but I am not pleased, content with my body,
until it is consumed or beneath another.
My best happiness comes after racquetball
and unsuccessful sex, the quiet self-righteous
thump of my heart, the fresh tone of my skin.

In retrospect you can say that it is unhealthy to be still—
that it is close to lethargy, that it is close
to old age which is close to death, that it is isolating.
And in retrospect you can say the same thing about motion—
instability, lack of focus, and a similar and confusing isolation.

16

Our lives begin and begin in such disconcerting ways.
I go to the doctor who says the same thing every year.
I try to floss, I try to exercise, I take up jogging,
but am more interested in inventing sandwiches.
I find pleasures but am upset with my satisfaction.
I want to come up with a phrase that will express how I feel about life.
One I can put on my dashboard, one that will help me to sleep.
I think about it often and realize it's a problem.

Once I woke up blue as a liver
my neck swollen and sensitive.
My mother said to move the hell out
before the place kills me
so I drove to Canada and slept in the car.

In a fevered way we become comfortable with our surroundings.
I was mad at the neighbors, their cat smelling up everything,
but drove them to the laundry and the supermarket anyway.

A bird hits my car, catches in the grill,
and I get nervous, pump the gas
and the brakes, a little dance
down the middle of Main Street
until I realize what I'm doing.

My grandmother would have said
I was just mortified and left immediately.
So I fly out of there and onto the highway,
the bird never lifting, never covering the window
with its dead expression, and after a half an hour
I'm home, doing the same stupid dance,
back and forth in the middle of the kitchen.

17

Maybe you don't know how a new apartment works.
You wake up and the toaster is on
the strange warm pulse of a past lover
turning the counter into the impression of a forearm
and heating up glasses with the memory of lips.

No alarms in a new place like this
so expect toast to wake you
blowing out all its blackness
and expect a strange taste to not ever go away.

18

I have broken down.
My sense of what it takes to be comfortable
having left apologetically.

I walk around until it is morning
and get the times from a drug store.
Fall asleep two blocks from the beach
one leg in the way of a bakery.
Some tiny percentage of sand in the street

the infrequent sound of waves
unmistakably, salt in the air (only a little)
but the sky is just the same
light as if you were flat out
in the middle of the ocean
boards tied together
nowhere to sleep but on my back
balance becoming surprisingly and fearfully important
and no one going to lean over me
in any way, just the seamless
cotton fabric of sky.

19

Day comes
moves through a deep blue brush of flowers
growing on grass in a dense and uneven pattern.

Not in one night
not just in one place.

Sand leaves my body
the entire walk home.

20

Funny
but there it goes
my life flashing before my eyes
each bit of happiness a film
adding a limb to the picture
a bubbling heated confusion

and I begin to understand how people wake up
alone or together, how they walk through a town.

I note the sound of a woman
the wood of her shoes
moving from one far away
to a very different far away.

Now the sun wants in
and an older man's voice grows clear
with the spotted yellow sounds
of becoming awake.

My car, piece by piece
is taken away by swift young men
who treasure it, the way you'd treasure a lung
the life returned to it, its every part embraced
as water returning to clouds is naturally embraced.

I do not wish for last words with my car, a last ride in my car.
The imperfection of the world becomes clear.
The squareness of signs. The laziness of animals.
The loud open quality of strangers
who've known each other for years.

Cars move by and in their presence
their bright red physicality
I believe them to be the greatest
smoothest, most natural things ever.

There is no one to tell me this
but everything's going to be all right.

The Redwoods: A Tragedy

FOR SETH KOEN

1

Leaves everywhere
and everywhere things
are bleached and yellow
the bushes
so many of them
trimmed, squared
and at one in the morning
it was a whole other year
the grass, fluorescent
the magic, flat
and left to itself
I can see San Jose
through the trees
every few minutes
a plane takes off
(always white)
are you getting the picture
of a place that is too quiet
without you
well the trees
break off at night
with a wonderful cracking
and any number of people
walk through the gravel
with dogs and on bicycles
the sun moves everything around
already today I have seen it
in the morning and twice
in the afternoon
I want to tell you

about the lamps
and the cup
and about everything
in this tiny
cream-colored place
but the room grows small
and at night it is easy
to become tired
and to sleep.

2

Oranges and redwoods
and orange trees
with people
on their way
one mountain
meaning as many mountains
as you want
and hundreds
of scraps of peeled wood
there is a place to clean my shirts
which I am doing
because it's four o'clock
in two hours company
will come
and it will be dark
you must remember
the olive trees
leaves like coins
brightness
turning a sunny face

in every direction
last night I could see
one of the dippers
from the patio
the air was cold
and I thought
this is darkness
the other house
had all its lights on
and I looked inside
from the lawn
I would suggest
the same for you
and for anyone.

3

I know you want
to hear about the redwoods
they wouldn't be anything
without the light
they grow in
even numbered groups
which might not be true
but I saw four
then I saw six
I also saw eight
but one was leaning in
I think that's in
and one from the six
was wrapped all the way
over a path

the bend
like your finger
so I won't go back there
under odd trees
like that
but I want to talk
about the redwoods
which split
like matches
or anything wooden
I was going to say
a table leg
but everything breaks
pretty much the same
saw a guy cleaning
his house at night
the lights on
I am drying
my shirts
as we speak
(whites)
only have four
and am wearing one
people might come
for dinner
my socks are there too
and it's getting dark here
and in the woods around here
the guy was sweeping
and listening to music
if you read this in the sun
it will be about the redwoods

and if you read this in the night
it will be about the man.

4

Three lawns worth of grass
and sometimes you go outside
and everything is wet
all the rocks and not under the cars
also there is a city eight miles away
I have counted six orange trees
and taken from two
the water must get on them
I mean each of the oranges
I cooked soup
and used half of one
then sat outside
where it was wet again
ate my soup
and didn't remember any rain
even now don't remember any rain
but there have been two days worth
isn't that funny
heard things being left by birds
noticed the purple
of nuts fallen on the road
more than once
(two kinds of purple)
but no rain
such a queer thing
with all this water.

5

It is only three busses
and an hour and a half to San Jose
and three busses
an hour and a half
and a hill back
sometimes I walk
two miles to town
(both ways)
most mornings
it is dark when I leave
and hot when I return
(uphill)
people were over
and could all hear the creek
through dinner
said things like
the creek sounds like a river
and how do you like to live
by a river
which I don't,
sad and cut my hair
in San Jose
you can see
San Jose from here
at night
didn't think
I could
or would ever
like the barber's job
so much

but no one
said anything
noticed I had cleaned the place
noticed I had enough glasses
noticed the creek
which sounds
like a river
I just realized
though they have said it often
and everyone left dinner
at the same time
you must have noticed
that before
then I heard the creek
and wished I could hear it
sounding like a creek.

6

What came down the river
besides turning bellies of water
were chunks of gold
first like nickels
then like paperweights
the size of cigarette boxes
or little fists
also the trees have peeled
down to the wax
of their single-boned bodies
are hard and distant
much more beautiful
than I remember

also the orchard
is full of trees
no apples
but full none the less
also the river
waits in spots
goes slow in spots
the prickers surround
the orchard
the bushes grow thickly
at the top of at least two peaks
and the lights of San Jose
take up most of the skyline
through implication
but what happens at night
is that the water
continues to run
the trees whipped
by something fantastic
crack and end up
in the lap of the morning
the chill takes an invisible
year off every quiet arm of the orchard
and you go to sleep
the lights of San Jose
so wild and unpredictable
that your sleep is spotty
and terribly unspecific
fearing that quality
of morning
so bright

so unaccountable
so far away.

7

Your dream
a narrative
your body
a pipe
hard and flat out
over the head
the redwoods appear
first from below
then from below again
then back to the narrative
pipe dream
of a walk
in the woods
just you and
(back again)
thin red trees
mostly white and sap
where the sun comes in
then you have barely taken a step
when the narrative drives off
like a rocket out of a bottle
dripping pepsi down a tree
your tongue
your tree
your forest
some little let in of light
no path

no way
more redwoods
and more redwoods.

8

You do not know
how many redwoods
if you were in the middle of them
you would still not know
you would think
I am in the redwoods
and don't know how far to go
you would look up
think something like
that's a quarter-mile up
think that's far
think a war could start
a quarter-mile away
think you'd never know
a war is good to explain
first a shot in the air
(you don't know why)
then an eye on the bullet
like a tail or like a kite
to some dirt patch
all dismissal and disintegration
in an inch and a half
but that's dead for a bullet
that dead is how tall trees are
white bodies above you
tall as trees

and you a bullet
slipped into the ground
head first
and you don't know
where you are
so many redwoods
so tall
so white.

9

Picture three paths
maybe four
first you see them like planets
shown over the years
on a map
but then they are wrangled around
like arms on the elbow
first they are the simple explanation of the day
then they are light blue night
like dolphins
or like the moon
two steps in front of you
picture my house
is a matchbox
that simple
a hundred little fingers
clearing the way
no shadows
and space
maybe you should think
of a houseboat

the water
something like all the lights
turned off
only ten o'clock here
but it's been dark long enough
I read three short lectures
two about how to listen
and another one
made the bed
did the dishes
ate again
this time bananas with honey
listened to the radio
made two calls
got one
a wrong number
for Allison
that I tried to draw out
and became a wrong number
for Ellen and Allison
have you lost sight of the house
or is it still
remember it is
on the water
it purrs like an animal
from here you see the woods
let out
white streams
mountain veins
and at night
it is even less
a number of paces

something you remember
in the day the trees are giant
today I gave one a name
I swore it would fall
I tried to imagine
the quarter-mile of damage
it would do
and couldn't
it was a thin thing
like a bat but still
how it might come down
on tiptoes
faster and faster
some tree
and from anywhere else
it is really just a stick of a thing
a toothpick
if you didn't know it well
after four hours of night
how much a tree can grow
how great a shadow it can project.

10

Two nights in a row
the back half of the forest unpeeled
like an orange
like something with a game on the mouth
like both halves of a joke
still connected
just watched
from the window

too dark to join the fun
just sat waiting
for the trees
to roll down
for something to knock
on the door
maybe night
maybe stars
maybe someone
who just learned
about fire
but nothing
just a little bit of smoke
a little bit of tea
the heater turning on and off
the place still staying cold
and when I came out of the bath
even less
and I didn't want to read
just thought about the trees
couldn't crack the trees
couldn't make the trees
couldn't find my way
through the forest
even if I had the sweaters for it
thought something about the telephone
and something about the mind
thought about all this sitting
thought about bringing the phone
to the bedroom
and to the bathroom
one phone

and I seem to bring it
everywhere
seem to act silly about the phone
bring it everywhere
when I'm in the woods
think about baiting wrong numbers
not getting off the line
think about the trees
some bark at the bottom
they are redwoods here
and I think about the tall ones most
about climbing them
like a monkey
until the skin of the tree is smooth
imagine that it is calm
towards the top
but it is probably not
it is quiet and dark in the house
and it is twelve
so I think
that there is culture
at the top of trees
that there is some kind of
monkey walk-around culture
don't really think that
but think I would be up there
and the phone would ring
could be you
could be my mother
could be someone who wouldn't call back.

First I find myself
in the kitchen
every five minutes
eating cookies
think that's not so bad
only eat one at a time
then think that's twelve an hour
and then they're gone
find myself in the cold
bedroom, in the tub
back in the kitchen
and in everything I do
the way I set the chairs
do two or three of the dishes
think about dinner
and open the refrigerator
go through with one hand
eat yogurt
then eat leftovers
and know that I am not hungry
the whole time
not sure how wrong this is
I know it's wrong
just don't know how bad
work for ten minutes
what couldn't have even been ten
open the fridge again
find nature
lettuce leaning down like a waterfall
two bad carrots

and a lemon that's gone brown
pull that stuff out
and now it is my own
particular kind of nature
there in the refrigerator
some staring white nature
about yourself
so much
the grapes seem bad
and now there is nothing
on the bottom shelf
but half of an orange
a slab of plastic
some light you can't trick
emotions dripping out
of the ice box
a breeze
through the back of your shirt
some crack in the window
and no joke I start eating the orange
despite what I've been thinking
about self control
and no way to end this
but it is still light
and there is water
two cans of pepsi
maybe nine or ten carrots
mushrooms
green beans
some fresh basil
there is chicken
there is garlic

there are a few things in little containers
and a few tomatoes
now it is starting to be dark
a little bit of cheese
a white onion
half a lime
three eggs
an artichoke and
yes and that's it
it's dark in the house
there is no one here
the windows have gone to mirrors
the floor has gone to sand
the kitchen opens up
like the side of a mountain
a flood of light
an echo
the staring promise
of something completely hollow.

Winter's Horizon

Returning
          to where you are
                through mist
        through everything
              and where you are
                is a small porch
        on a small island
                with a telephone
                its tiny open mouth
                    always there
                        if you concentrate
                            you will hear
                                a voice
                    within you say
                    (a maternal surety to it)
            that if you try
                        and you will try
                    you can expect
                        a not inglorious
              moderation
                      from the rest
                  of your life
and so as the poem begins
we visualize my father released
from burden, difficulty disappearing
as tension might wonderfully from a back
and it is this year's justice which we,
taking our own tiny role in the poem
may enact through sympathy, not pity,
and through the desire ourselves to be more grounded
as if the train tracks of our lives
were not quite meeting up

and the damn thing would just stop all the time
which give or take so many years' worth of specifics
is what our lives have been doing these days
and when you look at the world
                    what I want
                            is a backyard
                                    for you to see
                        a backyard
                yellow
                        healthy
                        crab grass
                green grass
                    realistic
                my father
            a ride-around
                        lawnmower
                    beneath him
                    let him go
                        let him go
                            the rain
                        rain for days
                            rain that is hard
                        purposeful rain
                    ceaseless rain
                            rain that speaks
                        says I won't stop
                            I won't stop
The whole family so down we are just looking at our shoes
and then a noise like the Russians
have finally attacked
                    inspired father
                    yellow sun

                    starting up
                 in the garage
                      appearing on its own
            God bless your father
        everyone runs quickly
                                        to the porch
                 pushing at the mesh windows
            our bodies waving good-bye
            God bless our father
            God bless him
                    and God bless
                the two thousand dollar
                bit of security
                        that motors him around
and when, after years, we finally fall in love
with the little places we have made it to
we live in them and describe them as islands
as pots of water coming to boil
contained and different, physical, obvious,
surrounded surrounded.

People who live on islands are a curious
caught up with themselves kind of people.
When they think about the future
they are a bit out of control
like every little thing
is life or death.
All anxious about the weather
as if it only happens in their little
middle of the ocean spot.
You've never seen so many people
say what the hell am I going to do

with my life, when am I gonna
get off this island,
and the mainlanders have a real
puppy-dog sensibility about the whole thing,
think it's just the greatest, how you can have
everything in the world pulled right up next to you.

Trees. Stone walls running haphazardly through woods.
A town filled with family, filled with classic worthwhile
education, filled with successful perennial plants,
when what we need is a landscape with more optimism.

You are young, maybe twelve, you write a story.
Your mom wants to know exactly what does it mean
for a kid to write a story about his father off and riding
the lawnmower into the sunset. You are puzzled by your own affection
for the story, but will fight her, saying "This story is great.
This story is full of meaning." She will think then,
and reflect later, on children's absurd little ways
of poking their heads right into the middle of the meanings
of everything. Adamancy and value clinking around
in their unspent thoughts. So powerful.
Little baby-thief, little danger-baby, so wise,
so nonchalant about knocking an entire cup of apple juice
on your sister and the rug. Your little stories
spreading out and staining the place.
Believable little apple juice stain
taking the form of fathers
banding and disappearing together
of mothers buried in the unkempt hair
of poorly attended lawns
of children settling into their little cribs of experience

growing old and wise on milk and on children's cookies
having sink-to-the-bottom perfectly sleepful dreams.

Splendid little
          ice water stream
      reflecting
    scales of fish
        over sand
            over rocks
      over what is brown
              and what is yellow
          through banks
              and bends
                and beds of
        fine river grass
                past neighbors
                    the tangled script
          sticks of growth
                    above you
                a tiny line
                        stays clear
            transparent
            intuitive

Within the garden's period of unraveled self-concerned discontent
Within its cluttered unconscious overgrowth
Something follows itself through a split in the yard
like a perfect ink line
like a pitcher held optimistically
and steadily above a tiny row
of hidden ungrown plants
pouring out a rain

that is wealthy and tiny and tender
but a boy of any age can read the message
of a lucid father loud and clear, steaming through
the brush of a family's little world
a fine and organic carpeting trailing behind
and a mother who talks about reality and fantasy,
who in broad terms has tried to fill you with responsibility,
begins to hold a very weak hand against the line-up
of this immediate new start of the imagination.

While meditating things will come into your mind and you
will want to clear them away, believe that they are fish
and your mind, a pool that longs to be vacant.
There is no use (you will go crazy) trying to keep fish
from your waters, so what you must do instead is draw them in
and with a calmness and a smoothness and a touch of their own
momentum, get the little trouble-fish (fish of what someone said
at work, fish of your family falling apart on the phone)
to move swiftly by, like a hand goes through the middle
of a pour from a faucet of water, the flow
seeming relatively undisturbed.

Your mother stares out
of the fuzzy police-camera part of your brain,
says look, I was just waiting for the fucker to come back.
Sure it was funny at first, ha ha, but come on.
I start thinking we've got half a dozen kids
and yell yell yell the next thing I know
I'm hypnotized
Stuff shooting out of the side
Grass looking new as Christmas
My man inching away

The wake closing like something at the end of a movie
and I start thinking the most honest
sort of cherishable thoughts
like how I love all you kids
enough to send you off that way
and how the beautiful circumstances
of grass washing after
of trails leading towards
will make easy
all the difficult
comings and goings.

We get into an uncompromising knot about the future.
I found myself telling my little sister
as she learned to drive
that she was thinking too much.
The older you get the more you believe in trust
and the less able you might actually be to do it.
I tell my sister to breathe and picture,
without even the slightest bit of cynicism
those firm bodied women on daytime television
who lift their arms and let them down
lift them and let them down
lift them and breathe
and let them down
my wonderful imagination
like waves
like summer
like anesthesia
but my reality is more like
my sister feeling great about things
for a minute, then nicking the curb,

then slamming the brakes, then continuing on
assuring me that she is breathing
she is breathing.

A garden feels nourished.
Its flowers open with directness and excellence.
At every point they present themselves with grateful postures
and the action of their end is the hand slipping gently
to the carpet, from the chest, from the leg, from the bed.
This is the sort of peace we ask for
and the sort of peace, at times, we deserve,
but you buy the kid a cheap sweater because what the hell
he's going to outgrow it in six months anyway
and the next thing you know he's just an inch too close
to the fire and fwoom, a kind of harmless flash from every
little loose end runs from bottom to top of him
and then goes out just as quick
scaring the hell out of his well-meaning three-year-old brother
who chases him around the room
just trying to get the damn sweater off.

The thing I like best about having once been a child
is the fireplace. It gets boring watching your father
push on towards Massachusetts, turning into a tiny little dot,
so you go inside and warm your cute little marshmallow toes
which seems perfectly reasonable and you have a three-year-old
twin brother to whom it seems perfectly reasonable as well.
When you are older the painting will be of a glass door
that stands eight feet by ten feet, between the porch
and the living room. On the porch a mother freezes
while her little boys, having locked the door, wrestle

with man's magic gift and then start hitting each other
with old Time magazines.

Dead
   unreceptive
      sound
         of the heart
         of people saying
             to themselves
          things like
            what the hell
          can be done
             and what the hell
          can be done
         from so far away
Soupy silence
       at 20¢ a minute
     piling up
       so much leaning
      so much flimsiness
      so much trust
          spread out
            thin as plastic
       and the phone
         accepts a very visual
      sort of distance
The help you look for when calling is the fisher
The phone, afloat on the kitchen table, is the buoy
The receiver and you are the fish and hook
                  the thin
               invisibility
             of wires

                                        connecting
                                    everything
                                        calm
                                    continuous
                                            uncaught
                                        scene
                            no tug
                                no tackle
                    simple giving up
                        simple going to lunch
                            simple scene staying simple
                                floating helplessly
                                    there forever

If you were a scientist
you would understand things differently
the macrocosmic and the microcosmic
would not blur and blend together
they would intertwine like rope
like wild prickered bushes
and you would see shoots
coming from shoots
defensive little marks
growing from their sides
you would watch them twist
in, out, and grow together at places
you would understand the soil
filled with particular vitamins
particular chemical memory
the tiny threads of grass
growing there
even and unnoticeable

beneath the turmoil of everything else
and all of this is not to say that you wouldn't
just go right ahead and mow the lawn like everyone else
but just that you might feel more fantastic
about doing it, might be more clear sighted
about the occurrence of change
but you did not
and I did not
and Jason
trying
drove
the thing
eight feet
into the woods
and sat there for an hour
The crack of bent twigs regaining their stature
The sound of failure whipping back into place
The wooden smack of history growing through the machine
for however many years we left it there.

The house, as much as you can say it will always stand,
is a wonderful thing. I kept aging and coming back
and then one day my sister said buy your mother plants
you know she works very hard to keep this place looking nice
and the stream in back would flow one year with cold clear water
and the next would come over the side revitalizing
the lush inappropriate skunk cabbage
would look like giant flowering heads of lettuce
would disappear beneath trees.

The boy gets an A+.
The teacher thinks it's a great story.

The mother wants to know why the hell everyone is so happy
with the father's little stunt, is upset with the teacher
for giving that kind of a grade, knows it's just a story
but wants to tell the kid not to listen to the teacher any more
and this is a very simple situation
a picture whose physicality begins with the house,
solid and durable, the people in it, frantic like ants,
but not so bad, human, a bit confused with their lot.
A man comically and dramatically escaping from the house
beginning a slow awkward and not so professional race
(we want to say towards something
but that would be pushing it)
so instead we say away from a house that is burning
like a big stack of leaves, smoke billowing out
in appropriate and tragic fashion
but what if instead of the house
it is the worn hand
the regular hand
coarse and burning
from a lit cigarette
the smoke from it
uncontrollably coming
with a hecticness
I've called humanness
instead of left to fill the sky
with a strange intangible grayness
consumed in a way like swallowing
filling the soft plumbing of the body
with a peppery mist
that if we understand air
to be freedom or nothing
would resemble something.

If a grown man on a porch
smoking and talking
on a telephone
to a family
that will not listen
watching the interior of his house
fold in on itself becoming darker and denser
as the outside does the very same thing
does not explain itself then remember
how you as a child first held a yo-yo
in your palm and threw it forcefully down

                              and how it
                    at the end
                        of its string
                      spun unbelievably fast
                          and at that moment
                        it seemed to be
                                  the subject
                        of the situation
                  but now you must
                            think visually
                      away and back
                  its size
                      its action
                            dwarfed
                    step back
                  by the size
                      the action
                        within
                    the smallest bodies
                          of children
                        as they run

                                          their minds
                                      racing on
                          as time-lapse photography
might show them growing up very quickly
                                  their thoughts
                              peddling out
                        in unstoppable
                              radiant ways
                                  until perfect
                                      flesh colored life
                                          looks around

This seems a bit too confessional
but did you ever get so scared you couldn't sleep
thinking everyone in your family was dead?
You all alone and the problem with the dream
is that it's not just that stranded-island
left-all-alone cry cry cry dream, it's worse
about people who hear and how they hear and
what has happened to you becomes a drunk public mess
with people confiding a special ultra-sensitized
version of your life and goddamn if anyone could
live like that, people just breaking down
with understanding at the sight of you.

First what can happen
is that they just take the kids away.
You are manic and unfit.
You provide the children with a poor example.
You are trying hard, but trying is simply,
obviously not enough.

There is a fantasy alive in your world
that is not alive in other places.
Your children are poorly prepared and poorly clothed.
They come to lunch without lunch.
They do not brush.
Their complex second grade society
knocks them around like fish following whales.

The sky opens up with an odd blueness.
You move to the window and then the porch.
You are hanging out the window
like the masthead of a houseboat
pushing into a rolling expanse of sky.
Unaged Columbus, you have left the kids
to the hot empty living room
where they dance around
like match sticks
knocking each other with every little jump.

In just a handful of years
my life has gone from falling apart
to put back together to falling apart
to put back together to falling apart
and it is not just what they say, every year
you *do* get another chance.

A man fell in love with me
and my daughter, who has become womanly
in a single day, says that all the boys think
they are in love with her, but they are not
and possessing too much of the beautiful

I suggest to this man that he is not
in love with me.

Convincing and becoming convinced is so easy,
but where exactly do you put everything.

Girl, I say, it's just you and me
not any goddamn promise on the telephone.

You see, everyone wants to do everything.
The house wants to be the burning house
its boards tarring up in the middle of
a perfectly manicured bright green lawn,
but it also wants to be sturdy and brick,
the hot unburnable live forever house
and the kids,
they want to be snowmen
one day bright and solid as ice
the next, half melting into the ground,
helpless and pressing
they want to be gone
into the river
or thrown at others
so malleable
they could cover mountains
with their futures
and it is disheartening
but parents want that very same thing
that wideness, that jump to disappearance
and just for the life of them
can't have it
no matter what sort of games

they start playing
no matter what
great eclipsing expanse
of night sky
they wander out into
no matter how breathless
or full of life they feel.

All too answerable songs
                    ricocheting off
                        a million little arms
                            extending from trees
                                forming fabulous features
                            of wild life
                                echoing back
                                    the breath
                                        as it runs out
                                    on itself
                                        as it returns
                                    to the front door
                                        of its darkness
                                    as its tracks evaporate
                                        into the fog
                                    easily settling
                                        back to earth
                                which purrs and sounds
                                    for far too long
                                like an engine
                        steadily moving away
                    until it is a thin line
                of reverberation
until you can no longer hear it

and its being gone
gives you a terrible sense
a terrible sense of completeness
a terrible sense that things like this
will continue to happen.

Joshua Beckman was born in
New Haven, Connecticut, and earned
his bachelor's degree from Hampshire College,
where he studied poetry and the art of the book.
He is the recipient of grants from the
Edward Albee Foundation, the Montalvo Center
for the Arts, and the Ludwig Vogelstein
Foundation, and has taught at Rhode Island
School of Design and Hampshire College.
He lives in Brooklyn, New York,
and works for Time Magazine.